FRIENDS NOT FOOD

THE LITTLE BOOK OF
VEGAN WISDOM

sphere

First published in Great Britain in 2019 by Sphere

Copyright © Little, Brown Book Group 2019
Written by Alison Griffiths
Designed and typeset by EM&EN

10 9 8 7 6 5 4 3 2 1

A CIP catalogue record for this book is available from the British Library.

ISBN 978-0-7515-7866-9

Printed and bound in Italy by L.E.G.O. S.p.A.

Papers used by Sphere are from well-managed forests and other
responsible sources.

Sphere
An imprint of
Little, Brown Book Group
Carmelite House
50 Victoria Embankment
London EC4Y 0DZ

An Hachette UK Company
www.hachette.co.uk

www.littlebrown.co.uk

'Animals are my friends,

and I don't eat my friends.'

George Bernard Shaw

Pigs were the first animals to be farmed. The earliest known book on pig farming was written by Chinese Emperor Fo Hi in 3468 BC.

EAT

BEANS

NOT

BEINGS

PLANET EARTH:

WE'RE ALL IN

IT TOGETHER

We share 60% of our
genes with chickens,
70% with zebrafish and
80% with cows.

Wild chickens naturally lay just ten to fifteen eggs per year and can live for six years. A farmed chicken might produce three hundred eggs per year but will usually be slaughtered after twelve to eighteen months of laying.

One glass of

fortified soya milk

a day gives you the

EU recommended amount

of Vitamin B12

Good night

Soya in the
morning

Studies have shown that
a plant-based diet can
reduce the risk of illness —
better for you, better
for the world!

A person who eats meat
could eat over 7,000 animals
in their lifetime.

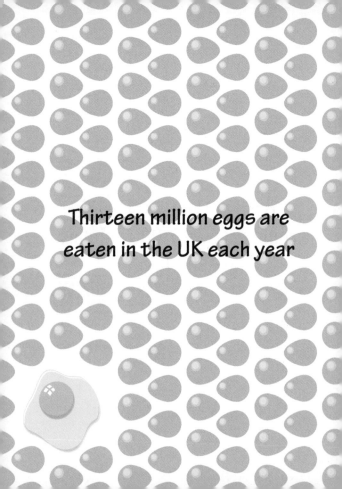

Thirteen million eggs are eaten in the UK each year

MY BODY IS A TEMPLE, NOT A TOMB

HAPPY COWS

JUMP FOR JOY!

BUT WHEN DID YOU

LAST SEE A COW

JUMPING?

'Animals, whom we have made our slaves, we do not like to consider our equal.'

Charles Darwin

Animals are here with us, not for us

VEGANS HAVE

GREAT TASTE

Going vegan cuts your
carbon footprint
by up to 73%

20,000 tons of octopus

are caught in Europe every year.

THERE ARE

TWENTY-FIVE BILLION

CHICKENS

IN THE WORLD.

The oldest recorded chicken was named Matilda. She lived to be sixteen years old — that's over twice the age of an average chicken.

GO NUTS!
Eight walnut halves
= your daily portion
of Omega 3

I heard that vegans will work for peanuts.

Well, they need the protein.

Only 3% of the planet's water is fresh water. It's a precious resource and we need to use it wisely.

Vegan diets save water!

- 1kg tomatoes = 214 litres
- 1kg potatoes = 287 litres
- 1kg apples = 822 litres
- 1kg cheese = 3,178 litres
- 1kg pork = 5,988 litres

'The more helpless a creature,

the more entitled it is to

protection by man from

the cruelty of man.'

Gandhi

BE KIND
TO EVERY KIND

If everyone went vegan,
we'd only need a quarter
of the current farmed land
in the world.

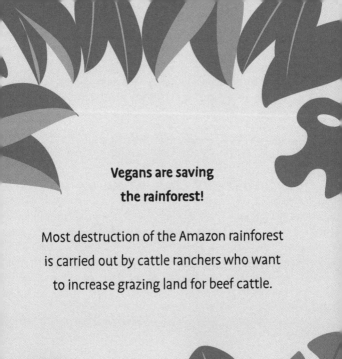

**Vegans are saving
the rainforest!**

Most destruction of the Amazon rainforest
is carried out by cattle ranchers who want
to increase grazing land for beef cattle.

Lobsters can grow up to

120cm long and live

up to a hundred years

Taking honey doesn't harm the bees, right?
Wrong: the sugar substitute that bee farmers
give them in return doesn't have the same
essential micro-nutrients that honey does.

AVOID HONEY:

BEE HAPPY!

'*I am in favour of animal rights as well as human rights. That is the way of a whole human being.*'

Abraham Lincoln

HUMMUS SAPIENS:

THE NEXT STEP ON THE

EVOLUTIONARY LADDER

Sheep can recognise

up to fifty other sheep and

remember them for two years.

NO BLOOD ON

MY HANDS

A pound of flesh is dearly bought.

Producing 1 lb of beef takes:

- 2,400 gallons of water
- 200 square feet of destroyed rainforest
- 36 kg of greenhouse gases emitted

'I am fond of pigs.

Dogs look up to us.

Cats look down on us.

Pigs treat us as equals.'

Winston Churchill

Only domesticated pigs have curly tails:

wild pigs' tails are straight.

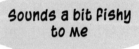

SOYA BEANS ARE 38% PROTEIN - HIGHER THAN CHEESE OR PORK.

Don't spill the beans!

Vegans need them

3,000,000,000,000 fish

are killed every year.

(That's three trillion,

if you were wondering.)

FOOTBALL BOOTS
LABELLED 'RKT'
ARE MADE FROM
KANGAROO SKIN.

Here's looking at ewe!

Everyone loves a celebrity sheep . . .

Shrek the Sheep hid in a cave
in New Zealand for six years until he
was finally caught and sheared.
His fleece weighed 27kg – an
average fleece is usually
around 4kg.

Wild turkeys can run at 25mph
and fly at 55mph.

Nine in ten of turkeys farmed in the UK spend their lives crammed into sheds of up to 25,000 birds.

I ONLY ROAST

COFFEE BEANS

A load of old lentils:
Lentils have been eaten since
Neolithic times and were one of the
earliest crops to be domesticated.
Archaeologists have found lentils in
Egyptian tombs dating back to 2400 BC,
and 8,000-year-old lentil seeds in
the Middle East.

A paddling of ducks . . .

a mob of sheep . . .

a drift of pigs . . .

a rafter of turkeys . . .

a farrow of piglets . . .

a hover of trout . . .

a pod of lobsters . . .

a covey of quail . . .

a cast of crabs . . .

a . . .

. . . kindness of vegans?

Healthy vegan diets can reduce the risk of obesity, stroke, type 2 diabetes, hypertension and some cancers.

Humans do not need cholesterol in their diets. High cholesterol can lead to cardiovascular disease. A vegan diet is cholesterol free!

When is a salmon not a salmon? When it's an alevin, char, chum, grilse, kelt, samlet, skegger, smolt or sprod.

It takes 500 wild-caught anchovies

to produce one farmed salmon

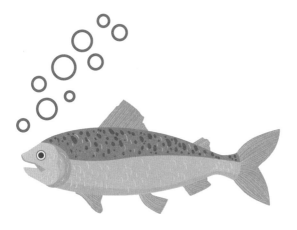

More chickens are
raised and killed for food
than all other land animals
combined.

'Never, ever be afraid

to do what's right,

especially if the well-being

of a person or animal

is at stake.'

Martin Luther King Jr.

Vegan irony:

Iron per 100g of beef: 2.6mg

Iron per 100g of dark chocolate: 11.9mg

SEAWEED SUPERFOOD!
NORI HAS 44% PROTEIN,
MORE VITAMIN C THAN ORANGES
AND AS MUCH B12 AS MEAT.

Pigs are seriously clever.

They can solve puzzles,

use a remote control and

play video games!

Out of every hundred calories
fed to animals, only ten to twelve
come back in their meat or milk.

Queen bees in commercial hives
have their wings clipped so they can't
fly away and start new colonies.

Be human

and humane

CHICKENS DREAM

Oysters are heroes of their ecosystem. They filter out algae and keep the water oxygenated for other aquatic life.

85% of the world's

wild oyster reefs have been

lost through overfishing

and pollution.

'Nobody really

needs a mink coat

– except the mink.'

Glenda Jackson

ANIMALS

ARE NOT

A FASHION

STATEMENT

Jumpin' jackrabbits!

Bunnies can really bounce.

The highest hop ever recorded

is 99.5cm by Mimrelunds Tösen;

the longest leap is 3m by Yabo,

both Danish. What do they

feed rabbits in Denmark?

The World's Biggest
Dish of Hummus was created
in 2010 in Beirut, Lebanon, and
weighed 10,452 kg! (They also had
to make the World's Biggest Plate,
measuring over 7 m across,
to serve it.)

VEGANS ARE ALWAYS

FULL OF BEANS

Fur is worn by
beautiful animals
and ugly people

Rabbits are the second most
farmed species in the EU.
Over 300 million are killed
for meat each year.

Is that a flying sheep?

A sheep, a duck and a rooster

made the maiden flight in the

Montgolfier brothers' pioneering

hot air balloon.

I'D RATHER HUG TREES

THAN MUG BEES

'Thus you bees make honey

not for yourselves.'

Virgil

THE GLOBAL EGG INDUSTRY
DESTROYS 6,000,000,000
NEWBORN MALE CHICKS
EVERY YEAR.

You TOTALLY CAN

make an omelette without

breaking eggs

Plenty more fish in the sea?

Atlantic cod: vulnerable

Haddock: vulnerable

Atlantic Bluefin tuna: endangered

'*By eating meat we share the responsibility of climate change, the destruction of our forests, and the poisoning of our air and water.*'

Thich Nhat Hahn

Eating a vegan diet for a year is a hundred times more effective at reducing emissions than giving up plastic bags.

Cows have feelings too.

Their two biggest fears are

falling and being alone. Cows make

special friendships and also

hold grudges against cows

that have annoyed them!

I've got a
tofu joke.

Don't bother,
it's bound to be
tasteless.

Legend has it that over
2,000 years ago, a Chinese chef
accidentally curdled some soya milk
with seaweed — thus inventing
the wonder food tofu!

NOT YOUR MUM:

NOT YOUR MILK

SOYA: THE MILK OF

HUMAN KINDNESS

Cows have a
great sense of smell.
They can smell something
up to 6 miles away.

Every two minutes, a whale, dolphin

or porpoise dies from getting

tangled up in fishing gear.

'Mankind's true moral test,
its fundamental test (which lies
deeply buried from view), consists
of its attitudes towards those who
are at its mercy: animals.'

Milan Kundera

SEVEN IN TEN MEAT CHICKENS ARE RAISED IN

INTENSIVE FARMS.

A FACTORY-FARMED CHICKEN HAS MORE SPACE

IN THE OVEN THAN WHEN IT WAS ALIVE.

It takes 10 litres of milk
to make 1kg of hard cheese.

WHO SAYS VEGANS
ARE HUMOURLESS?
WE JUST DON'T LIKE
CHEESY JOKES.

Wild turkey mums communicate

with their chicks in the shell and after

they are born. Farmed turkey chicks

never meet their mothers.

'My body will not be a

tomb for other creatures.'

Leonardo da Vinci

Ostriches are awesome!

Largest bird;

largest eggs;

fastest two-legged runner;

biggest eyes

of any land animal.

LOVE THE BIRDS

NOT THE BURGERS

Although cows can live to
the age of twenty, most of those
raised for meat don't make it
past two years old.

LIFE IS TOO SHORT
TO MAKE OTHER LIVES
SHORTER

Pigs snuggle close to one another and
like to sleep nose to nose.

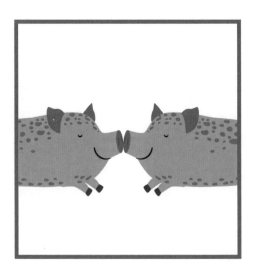

Unicorn pigs really exist! Well, existed.

An ancient species of pig living seven to twenty

million years ago had a large horn growing out

of its forehead — hence the name, unicorn pig!

Sheep are as clever
as cows and nearly as
clever as pigs.

In the dairy industry, calves
are taken away from their mothers
within twenty-four hours of birth.

'To every cow her calf.'

St Colum Cille, 6th century

Change is happening!
The production of foie gras,
involving cruel and painful
force-feeding of geese, has been
banned in the UK since 2000.

NO DESIGNER
SHOWED FUR
IN LONDON
FASHION WEEK
2018.

GEESE MAKE BRILLIANT PETS!

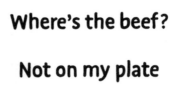

THERE'S NO SUCH THING AS

MAD CARROT DISEASE

Vegans eat a ton of veg
— but that usually involves
more than one vegetable.
The world's heaviest pumpkin
was grown in Belgium in 2016
and weighed in at 1,190kg
— just over a ton!

BEETS
NOT
MEATS!

Cows with names produce more milk.

How would you feel about working for

a boss who couldn't be bothered

to remember your name?

Geese mate for life and are

loyal to their partners. If its partner

or young ones are injured, a goose will

stay with them even when the rest of

the flock begin migration.

'The basis of all

good human behaviour

is kindness.'

Eleanor Roosevelt

Ducks' feet have no blood vessels so they can't feel the cold.

UK law does not require farmers to give ducks access to water, other than drinking water.

Britain produces 22,000 tons
of wool a year.

After ewe

Studies have shown
that vegan diets can reduce
insulin dependence
in diabetics.

SAVE YOUR BACON.

GO VEGAN.

The mushroom known as 'chicken of the woods'
actually tastes like fried chicken. So . . .
who needs to eat chicken?

Chicken chat: chickens are social birds and make at least twenty-four different sounds when they communicate.

A cow's main stomach can hold over 200 litres of partly digested grass!

CHOOSE VEGANISM.

CHOOSE COMPASSION.

'The love for all living creatures is the most noble attribute of man.'

Charles Darwin

According to the UN,

animal agriculture is

responsible for more

greenhouse gas emissions

than is transport.

VEGANS ARE
PART OF THE SOLUTION,
NOT THE PROBLEM

Crabs are blue-blooded!

Not because they're aristocrats;

it's the copper in their blood.

If everyone in the world
went vegan, we could cut
greenhouse gas emissions
by 70%.

VEGANS

COULDN'T

CARE

MORE

POWERED BY

PLANTS

'*The only way to have*

a friend is to be one.'

Ralph Waldo Emerson

EARTH

IS FOR

ALL OF US